Union Cemetery,Greenwich,Fairfield County,Conn.,

Copied by Mr.William A.Eardeley,
Post Office Box 91,Brooklyn,
New York   9 June 1907
and accurately compared Dec.,
4,1912

Notice

Union Cemetery, Greenwich, Fairfield County, Connecticut

Transcribed by:

William A. Eardeley

Originally published:
Brooklyn
1907

Reprinted by

Janaway Publishing, Inc.
732 Kelsey Ct.
Santa Maria, California 93454
(805) 925-1038
www.janawaygenealogy.com

2009

ISBN: 978-1-59641-173-9

Made in the United States of America

Union Cemetery,Greenwich,Fairfield County,
Conn.; still used ; well kept.

Copied by Mr.William A.Eardeley,
Post Office Box 91,Brooklyn,
New York,9 June 1907.

Alford   see Scofield 427

Ausborn   see Christian 70

  Allen   see Green 144
1.   Margaret d.10 July 1862 ae.69
2.   William d.29 Dec.1899 ae.77
3.   Caroline his wife d.28 Nov.1895 ae.68
4.   Maggie J_____ (Called "Nin") b.1853 d.1904 no
                more
5.   Thomas d.11 Apr.1860 ae.35
6.   Sarah Louise b.18 Dec.1862 d.28 July 1865
7.   Margaret Jane b.8 Aug.1847 d.7 Aug.1848

8.Armstrong   James H_____ d.22 July 1862 in 25

9.Adlay   Enoch d.20 Apr.1902 ae.37

10.Adsit   Fanny K_____ b.4 June 1848 d.21 Dec.1902 wife
                of Daniel H_____
11.   Archie D_____ b.30 June 1876 d.20 Sept.1905
12.   Violet b.6 Aug.-- d.27 Aug.-- 1881
13.   Helen S_____ b.12 Mch.-- d.23 Aug.-- 1875
14.   Frank K_____ b.2 Jan.1886 d.28 Jan.1888
                11 per 14 are the children of Daniel H_____
                and Fanny K_____

15.Anyan   Sergt.Lionel d.5 Aug.1877 ae.38 ; Company A first
                N.Y.Vol.Engineers

  Barnacutt   see Studwell 460

  Barremore   see Dick 85

  Belcher   see Mead 323 and 343

  Benedict   see Horton 173

Blackett   see Ritch 413

15a. Blake   B_____ G_____ no dates Co.D,107 Conn.,Inf.
15b.   G_____ W_____ no dates Co.B,93 N.Y.Inf.

16. Bloomfield Walter S_____ b.1 June-- d.19 Oct.-- 1886
17.   Joseph H_____ b.16 Sept.1884 d.24 June 1888
          16 and 17 are the children of Samuel and Margaret

Brooker   see Merritt 296

Brown   see Mead 336

Brush   see Dayton 101 ; Hobby 176

Buckhout   see Studwell 466 and 467

Bunker   see Studwell 453

Burns   see Owens 354

Bush   see Mead 243

Byrns   see Owens 354

18. Barremore Walter d.22 Apr.1825 ae.35-2-11 merchant of N.Y.

19. Brinkerhoff Abraham b.6 June 1816 d.11 July 1894
20.   Charlotte his wife d.8 Feb.1903 ae.77
        these two are on a monument

21. Burns   Erastus b.9 Apr.1830 d.4 Mch.1905 Company I 10
        Conn.,Vols.
22.   Sarah F_____ b.1858 d.1865 no more

23.Burns   Percy b.1860 d.1861   no more
24.   George H_____ b.1872 d.1880   no more
             12 per 14 are the children of Erastus and Lucy M__
25.   Sarah wife of Hiram b.1802 d.1889   no more
26.   Rebecca Miller wife of Eleazer Burns b.1804 d.1896
             no more
             21 per 26 are in a plot

27.Burns   Chloe d.28 July 1855 ae.78-4-17
28.   James d.28 Sept.1853 ae.79-6-22
29.   Lorain Hopper d.5 Dec.1852 ae.7 months daughter of
             Leander H_____ and Ellen M_____
30.   Richard d.18 Feb.1876 ae.78-3-23
31.   Mary his wife d.13 Mch.1864 ae.62-10-16
32.   Ephraim their son d.3 Apr.1852 in 24

33.Bush   Arthur b.12 May 1858 d.11 Aug.1885
34.   Candice d.11 Aug.1859 ae.80
35.   Hester Mead d.2 Mch.1864 ae.66 daughter of Candice
             Bush

36.Bancroft Harriet d.1 May 1871 ae.82

37.Banks   Edwin M_____ b.25 Nov.1862 d.16 Mch.1888

38.Barnes   Gertrude M_____ d.4 Aug.1892 ae.0-4-13 daughter of
             R_____ M_____ and Lizzie
39.   Josiah d.1 May 1868 ae.22-6-25
40.   Ida d.9 Jan.1868 ae.2-7-5

41.Bock   Adam b.1817 d.1886   no more
42.   Mary Pieffer his wife b.1820 d.1900   no more

43.Barmore   Jennie L_____ d.9 June 1878 ae.11-6-0 daughter of
             William H_____ and Elizabeth
44.   William H_____ d.15 Apr.1881 ae.56-2-0
45.   Rebecca F_____ his wife d.13 Jan.1857 ae.31-1-0
46.   Nathaniel d.1 Nov.1867 ae.66-10-0
47.   Nathaniel d.4 Oct.1863 ae.33

48.Barrell   Cornelius J_____ d.26 Nov.1861 ae.1-11-3
49.   Evveline d.9 Apr.1863 ae.0-10-17
             48 and 49 are the children of Hubbard C_____ and
             Mary A_____

Carleton   see Smith 442

Chandler   see Partridge 383

50. Chappel   Capt.Amos d.11 Mch.1777 ae.41 of Sharon,Conn.;
                commander in the expedition

51. Chase   Nathaniel S_____ b.7 Apr.1824 d.22 Sept.1898
52.   Eliza Sherwood his wife b.6 Aug.1834 d.4 Nov.1898
            these two are on a monument
53.   Ann Maria b.1851 d.30 Mch.1864 ae.12-5-23
54.   Emma C_____ b.1858 d.5 Jan.1862 ae.3-3-0
55.   Everett Sherwood b.1866 d.1 Oct.1868 ae.2-1-16
            53 per 55 are the children of 51 and 52
            51 per 55 are in a plot

Chester   see Talbot 477

Clark   see Mead 289 and 290

56. Carr   Emeline d.8 Jan.1865 ae.19-5-2 wife of Frank W_____
            Webb
57.   also Carrie their infant daughter no dates

58. Cameron   Ray d.28 Apr.1885 ae.1-6-0

59. Carpenter   Addie P_____ b.18 Dec.1863 d.7 Mch.1875 daughter
            of Nathan and Margery
60.   Nancy b.28 June 1857 d.13 Oct.1886 wife of B_____
            Farrington Hunt

61. Crawford   George A_____ G_____ b.8 Apr.1883 d.21 Feb.1891
62.   Jennie G_____ b.20 Sept.1873 d.25 Sept.1874
63.   James A_____ b.27 Mch.-- d.6 Sept.-- 1879
            62 and 63 are on the same stone
            61 per 63 are the children of William H_____ and
            Sarah

64. Carter   John W_____ b.19 May 1821 d.3 Oct.1890
65.   Eliza B_____ his wife b.20 Dec.1832 d.12 Apr.1895
66.   Maria S_____ Merritt d.3 Sept.1888 ae.80-10-22
            "Mother"
67.   Ebenezer Wright d.13 May 1851 ae.47-9-3

68.Carter   Deborah Wright b.9 Dec.1800 d.7 Dec.1890
64 per 68 are in a plot

69.Chard   William d.6 Apr.1873 ae.67-6-0

70.Christian William Henry b.31 May 1861 d.26 Oct.1875 ae.14-4-
-26 son of John Ausborn Christian and Eliza
71.   John Osborn b.Mch.__ 1829 d.6 Feb.1903
72.   Eliza Funston his wife b.31 July 1835 d.24 May 1895

73.Charman   Malvina d.2 July 1870 ae.15 years daughter of Henry
and Mary F_____

74.Chard   David B_____ b.19 July 1843 d.22 July 1891
75.   Ludlow L_____ d.6 Aug.1865 ae.24-6-16 formerly of
Company I 10 Conn.,Vols.

Delano   see Reynolds 389 and 390

76.Denton   Humphrey b.10 Oct.1821 d.13 Jan.1886
77.   Ruth M_____ Peck his wife b.24 Feb.1825 d.6 Jan.1857
78.   Catherine Kelly his second wife b.1 Feb.1840 nO more
these three are on a monument
79.   Lillian J_____ d.11 Aug.1880 ae.27-11-0 daughter of
76 and 77

80.Denton   Samuel S_____ d.16 July 1863 ae.34-11-22
81/   John M_____ d.26 Apr.1872 ae.77-2-23
82.   Elizabeth wife of Jabez d.16 Feb.1883 ae.87
83.   Samuel S_____ d.16 Feb.1874 ae.15-7-24
84.   Willie M_____ d.20 July 1883 ae.20-3-10
83 and 84 are the children of Samuel S_____ and
Margaret

85.Dick   Mary Barremore b.3 Jan.1794 d.1 Mch.1866

Drake   see Marshall 306 and 311 ; Studwell 451

86.Denton   Thomas C_____ b.1804 d.1888 no more
87.   Sally M_____ b.1813 d.1884 no more

88.Delano   Rufus C_____ d.6 Oct.1890 ae.63-0-26
89.   Mary his wife d.15 Sept.1883 ae.51

90.Darrow   no name b.12 Feb.1831 d.19 Nov.1858

91.Darrah   Jane d.10 Sept.1866 ae.40 wife of John
92.   Margaret b.18 Jan.1857 d.17 Feb.1873

93.takes the place of 15a
94.takes the place of 15b

95.Douglass   Kate b.26 Apr.1864 d.1 Apr.1866
96.   John b.24 Aug.1867 d.10 Sept.1868
                 95 and 96 are the children of Archibald and
                 Katherine

97.Danard   Agnes McFarland b.8 Dec.1875 d.28 Aug.1888
98.   Sarah Maria b.31 Aug.1847 d.1 Sept.1902 wife of
                 William

99.Doty   Cyrus B_____ b.5 Aug.1897 d.20 May 1900 dau-
                 ghter of Cyrus E_____ and Amelia

100.Dayton   David b.6 Mch.1798 d.26 Jan.1872 ae.73-16-20
                 son of David and Elizabeth (Osborn)
101.   Elizabeth Brush his wife d.20 Sept.1863 ae.66-
                 -7-8 daughter of Edward Brush
102.   David O_____ d.7 Mch.1866 ae.26-0-12
103.   Charles d.16 Jan.1881 ae.48-6-12
                 102 and 103 are the children of 100 and 101

104.Elliott   Jennie d.19 Nov.1869 ae.3-1-6 youngest daughter
105.   Georgeana H_____ d.10 Jan.1857 ae.10 days
                 104 and 105 are the children of J_____ D_____
                 and O_____ A_____
106.   Joseph K_____ d.10 May 1860 ae.0-3-5 son of
                 William and Mary A_____
107.   Nancy D_____ d.14 Sept.1848 ae.40 wife of Wil-
                 liam
108.   Mary Amanda d.24 Sept.1848 ae.26 days daughter
                 of William
                 107 and 108 are on the same stone

109.Eliot   Jane d.2 Nov.1883 ae.77 wife of William McDou-
                 gall

Everett   see Chase 55 ; Reynolds 389

Farrington	see Carpenter 60
Ferris	see St.John 419 ; Studwell 451
Finch	see Mead 347
Finette	see Mead 277
110.Ferris	Jacob d.4 Mch.1871 ae.60
111.Fraser	Anna S_____ d.7 Jan.1901 ae.71
Funston	see Christian 72
112.Ferris	Harvey L_____ d.14 Sept.1895 no age infant son of H_____ P_____ and E_____ S_____
113.	Maud Estelle d.6 Feb.1893 ae.13-10-0
114.	Laura Mabel d.17 July 1887 ae.0-11-15 113 and 114 are the children of George T____ and Estelle M_____
115.Field	Joseph C_____ d.30 Mch.1860 ae.31-0-28
116.Felmette	James d.22 Sept.1848 ae.46-3-13
117.	Elizabeth his wife d.9 July 1855 ae.52-5-0
118.Funston	Isabella d.8 Apr.1868 ae.41 wife of Hugh
119.	Sarah d.30 Sept.1889 ae.49 wife of Hugh
120.Foster	John E_____ b.3 Mch.1840 d.18 Aug.1901 G.A.R.
121.Ferguson	Nancy d.5 Dec.1874 ae.78 wife of William
122.	William Ray d.11 Oct.1893 ae.49
123.	Margaret his wife d.12 Aug.1877 ae.31 122 and 123 are on the same stone
124.	Robert J_____ Ray d.11 Feb.1887 ae.17 years 121 per 124 are on a monument and in a plot
125.Funston	James b.30 June 1848 d.13 July 1876
126.	Henry d.4 Aug.1893 ae.48-3-0

127.Funston   William d.9 Aug.1891 ae.51

128.Ferris   Clement E_____ d.17 Jan.1867 ae.0-4-11 son of
           J_____ and E_____
129.   John d.19 Mch.1871 ae.67
130.   Mary A_____ his wife d.9 Mch.1882 ae.74-6-0
           129 and 130 are on the same stone
131.   Alexanderd.16 May 1864 ae.21-5-0 at Drury's Bluff,
           Virginia in battle ; son of John and M_____ Amanda
132.   Elizabeth B_____ d.8 Dec.1834 ae.3-3-29
133.   Henry L_____ d.5 June 1849 ae.1-7-19
           132 and 133 are the children of John and M_____
           Amanda

134.Gibson   Alexander d.8 Mch.1877 ae.55-1-4

     Gilbert   see Marshall 329 and 332 ; Shute 435

135.Gelin   Pierre b.Angers,France 1797 d.1875 no more
136.   Marie Louise his wife b.Paris,France 1811 d.1876
           in Brooklyn,N.Y. no more

137.Garey   Lizzie C_____ ("Lill") wife of John W_____ b.1872
           d.1902 no more

138.Gibson   George W_____d.18 Sept.1877 ae.29-1-18

139.Green   Solomon H_____ d.20 Aug.1886 ae.76
140.   Lucinda his wife d.24 Nov.1886 ae.71
141.   Henry d.1 May 1869 ae.60
142.   Tempy his wife d.26 Apr.1879 ae.80
           141 and 142 are on the same stone
143.   George E_____ d.1 Dec.1875 no age Co.G, 29 Conn.Vols
144.   Allen d.13 July 1878 ae.74
145.   Mary his wife d.4 Feb.1879 ae.71
           144 and 145 are on the same stone
146.   Anna B_____ d.14 June 1877 ae.18-4-14

     Guernsey   see Peck 358

     Hamilton   plot ; no stones

     Hickson   see Merritt 258

147.Hobby   Joseph S_____ d.7 Dec.1898 no age

     Holly   see Moshier 349

     Hopper   see Burns 29

     Hoyt   see Smith 442

     Hudson   see Ritch 405

     Hugford   see Lent 206

     Hunt   see Carpenter 60

     Hyatt   see Studwell 457

148.Henderson a son d.22 Mch.1843 no age
149.   a son d.22 Dec.1851 no age
             148 and 149 are the children of John and Mary

150.Howard   Rachel b.25 Mch.1792 d.21 Nov.1866 ae.74
151.   Daniel d.1 June 1866 ae.66-1-29
152.   Hannah his wife d.21 June 1874 ae.70
153.   Althea b.30 Oct.1826 d.18 July 1900
154.   Margaret Jane d.6 May 1833 ae.4-1-0
155.   Henry Scudder d.26 May 1840 ae.1-10-0
156.   Hannah Maria d.10 Apr.1847 ae.3-10-0
             153 per 156 are the children of 151 and 152
157.   William b.28 Dec.1859 d.8 Jan.1892
158.   Amanda Florence his wife b.8 July 1864 d.8 Jan,1902
159.   William McF_____ b.28 Dec.1824 d.23 Mch.1883

160.Heady   Solomon aged 85 no more
161.   Diana aged 66 no more
             these two are on a monument

162.Hubbard   Henry d.15 Nov.1904 ae.74
163.   Isabella June his wife d.19 Jan.1901 ae.63
164.   Wallace Smith their son d.13 June 1867 ae.0-5-13

165.Hewes   Polly d.6 May 1876 ae.74-8-23

166.Hammell   William d.29 Aug.1854 ae.36

167.Hess   John d.5 Mch.1883 ae.1-8-7
168.   Elizabeth d.2 Nov.1874 ae.0-5-4
169.   John d.22 Dec.1874 ae.0-6-24
              167 per 169 are the children of John and Elizabeth

170.Hutchinson Thomas b.8 Aug.1810 d.26 Oct.1881   erected by his
              children

171.Hubbard   Charles d.24 Feb.1876 no age Co. H 28 Conn.Vols.

172.Hanthorn Martha d.12 Aug.1874 ae,38-1-0 wife of Robert

173.Horton   Frederick Benedict d.16 Sept.1858 ae.1-6-27 son of
              Henry D_____ and Sarah

174.Hecker   Frederick A_____ d.16 Jan.1901 ae.5-4-2 son of
              F_____ M_____ and L_____ R_____

175.Hobby   Hezekiah d.13 Nov.1837 ae.77 son of Col.Thomas
176.   Elizabeth Mead his wife b.Sun.29 Jan.1764 d.20 June
              1824 ae.60 daughter of General John and Mary (Brush)
177.   Mary E_____ B_____ d.4 Mch.1877 ae.76
178.   Cecelia E_____ B_____ d.26 Nov.1849 ae.17
              177 and 178 are on the same stone
179.   Samuel D_____ (M.D.)d.7 June 1861 ae.80
              177 per 179 are the children of 175 and 176
              175 per 179 are on a monument

180.Hobby   Clemence nee Hobby relict of Thomas d.13 Oct.1829
              in 77 daughter of Joseph and Sarah (Knapp) Hobby
181.   Jabez M_____ b.21 July 1780 d.14 Dec.1834 son of
              son of Thomas and Clemence (Hobby) Hobby
182.   Jerusha wife of Jabez M_____ d.12 June 1814 ae.27
183.   Jerusha their daughter d.4 Apr.1814 ae.0-10-7

184.Husted   Jane Ann d.16 July 1851 ae.22-2-11
185.   Helen d.2 Oct.1851 ae.52-2-11
186.   Lucy Park d.30 July 1796 ae.65-0-6 wife of Moses

187.Ingersoll Caroline nee Merritt or Scofield b.10 June 1817 d.
              10 Oct.1875 wife of Roswell R_____ ; he was son of
              Nathaniel and Abigail (Webber) Ingersoll

188. Jermon   George d.18 Sept.1865 ae.42-4-12
189.   Nancy his wife d.19 Mch.1902 ae.80-1-23

190. Johnson   Ulrica Spencer b.16 Nov.1901 d.2? Feb.1903

    June   see Hubbard 163 ; Lent 206 ; Studwell 454

191. Kalb   Margaret d.15 Apr.1884 ae.55-11-26 wife of John
192.   George b.14 Aug.1855 d.14 Sept.1857
193.   John b.20 July 1857 d.8 Sept.1862
    192 and 193 are the children of John and Margaret

194. Kane   Willie d.20 Jan.1858 ae.1-8-17 son of Henry and
    Matilda

    Kelly   see Denton 78

    Knapp   see Hobby 180

195. Knapp   Harriet A_____ d.6 May 1868 ae.34-3-5 daughter of
    William and Catharine
196.   William H_____ b.30 Mch.1817 d.24 Jan.1901
197.   Catherine A_____ his wife b.9 Oct.1817 d.5 Apr.1884
    196 and 197 are on the same stone

    Lambert   see Merritt 226

198. Lally   James A_____ d.27 Nov.1885 ae.33-0-14

199. Lent   Martha A_____ d.17 Dec.1883 ae.20 wife of Charles
    E_____

    Lewis   see Peck 359

    Lockwood   see Mead 289

    Ludlow   see Chard 75

    Lyon   see Mead 345

```
200.Lyon       Algernon   no dates
201.           David b.18 Aug.1813 d.30 Dec.1896
202.           Elizabeth M_____ his wife b.10 Aug.1816 d.11 Dec.1881
203.           William H_____ their son b.17 Dec.1855 d.3 July.1893
204.           Edith M_____ b.4 Feb.-- d.12 Aug.-- 1885 daughter of
               W_____ H_____ and Ella F_____
               201 per 204 are in, a plot


     Luther    see Peck 371 ; Studwell 451


205.Luther    Wilber d.19 Nov.1802 in 32     "A.F.and A.M."


206.Lent      Elijah b.17 June 1821 d.10 Jan.1892 ( he married Pru-
              ella Sherwood daughter of Hugford and Betsey June
              Sherwood )


207.Lombard   Joseph A_____ b.18 Aug.1835 in Boston,Mass.,d.14 Mch.
              1862 killed   Sergt.Co.  I 10 Conn.Vols.


208.Lockwood  Lilly May d.9 Aug.1874 ae.2-6-0
209.          Sydney Mills d.31 Jan.1876 ae.0-10-16


210.Lockhart  John d.3 Jan.1891 ae.68-7-0
211.          Jane his wife d.24 Mch.1887 ae.58-10-0
212.          Elizabeth d.14 Oct.1848 ae.20-6-0 wife of John
213.          Joseph d.11 Mch.1876 ae.51
214.          Catherine his wife d.17 Oct.1865 32-11-17
215.          Maggie d.5 Nov.1862 ae.2-4-11 daughter of Andrew and
              Annie


216.Lockwood  Oliver b.3 Oct.1831 d.3 Feb.1906
217.          Elizabeth his wife b.4 Dec.1840 d.23 Nov.1866


     Marshall see Stevens 447


     McDougall see Eliot 109


     McFarland see Danard 97


     Mead      see Bush 35 ; Hobby 176 ; Merritt 258 ; Moshier 349 ;
               Peck 364 and 380 ; Ritch 411
```

Merritt   see Carter 66 ; Ingersoll 187

Miller   see Burns 26

Mills   see Lockwood 209 ; Mead 291 and 339

218.Morrell   Ephraim M_____ b.22 June 1831 d.24 Apr.1900
219.   Emily C_____ b.4 Nov.1833 d.31 Dec.1903 "Mother"

220.Mead   Robert P_____ b.30 Jan.1824 d.29 Dec.1884

221.Mather   Thomas d.26 Apr.1863 ae.95-3-0
222.   Frances Aurelia d.28 Jan.1861 ae.18-5-5 daughter
                of A_____ E_____ and Frances

223.Morrell   George d.16 June 1895 ae.48
224.   Simeon F_____ b.8 May 1816 d.4 May 1888
225.   Elizabeth his wife b.2 Jan.1819 d.26 Sept.1877
                224 and 225 are on a monument

226.Merritt   Melicent d.7 Feb.1848 ae.29-1-0 wife of Abram
                daughter of James and Charity Lambert
227.   Elvina their daughter d.8 May 1848 ae.1-1-0

228.Morton   Rubindin S_____ d.7 Aug.1900 ae.16-5-0 son of
                Joseph and Mary

229.Morrell   Wallace P_____ b.8 Mch.1853 d.1 Sept.1906
230.   Charles d.19 Oct.1893 ae,84-8-10
232.   Julia his wife d.4 Nov.1900 ae.81
231.   Phebe his wife d.16 Sept.1851 ae.42-5-13

233.Mc Gurn   Margaret b.7 Feb.1788 d.22 Aug.1871 ae.83-6-15
234.   Matilda S_____ d.28 July 1849 ae.27-5-12 wife of
                William
235.   William Edward d.6 Aug.1867 in Shanghai,China ae.
                25-1-18 only son of 234
236.   Ann Amelia d.7 Sept.1848 ae.4 years
237.   Charles H_____ d.17 May 1856 ae.2-2-9
                236 and 237 are the children of 234

238.Mead   Amos b.6 Nov.1807 d.22 June 1885

239.Mead   Mary Eliza his wife b.18 July 1830 d.d.17 Feb.1883
240.   Joseph Warren d.27 Sept.1865 ae.0-8-12
241.   Ida Melissa d.27 Feb.1862 ae.0-11-21
             240 and 241 are the children of 238 and 239

     Morrell   see Turner 488

242.Mead   Matthew d.1 Dec.1873 ae.59-9-11
243.   Mary Bush his wife d.26 July 1863 ae.49-10-3
244.   Harriet Louisa their daughter d.24 Nov.1862 ae.9-1-2

245.Mead   William b.15 May 1816 d.20 Aug.1884
246.   Sarah A_____ his wife b.6 Jan.1828 d.16 May 1874
247.   their infant sons b.7 Feb.-- d.8 Feb.-- 1855

248.Marshall Hiram R_____ d.3 Mch.1879 ae.47-5-0
249.   Emily his wife d.22 Feb.1863 ae.26-11-22
250.   Emily F_____ d.14 June 1868 ae.14-3-26
251.   Olive Pond d.2 Aug.1862 ae.1-1-0
             250 and 251 are the children of 248 and 249

252.Merritt   John H_____ b.9 Mch.1827 d.10 Nov.1883
253.   Lucinda W_____ his wife b.13 Feb.1818 d.6 Sept.1899
254.   Willie L_____ their son d.22 Nov.1862 ae.2-3-22
255.   Daniel b.9 June 1803 d.9 Mch.1884
256.   Rachel his wife b.1 Sept.1803 d.30 May 1879
             252 per 256 are on a monument

257.Merritt Henry C_____ d.24 July 1862 ae.2-3-10 son of Henry
        B_____ and Theresa
258.   Hannah relict of Hickson d.26 June 1860 ae.69-11-10
        daughter of Matthew and Nancy Mead

259.Mills   Gertrude d.18 Dec.1879 ae.2 years (wooden)
260.   Samuel Herbert d.12 Feb.1882 ae.2-6-9 son of Samuel
        A_____ and Elizabeth

261.Matthews Charlie d.25 July 1884 ae.16-7-25 son of Charles
        C_____ and Sarah E_____
262.   William Henry d.6 May 1847 ae.8 days
263.   Matthew Henry d.18 Sept.1849 ae.1-0-8
            262 and 263 are the children of John and Susan

264.Manning	Delia wife of James b.1834 d.1889 no more	
265.	Willie F_____ d.24 May 1886 ae.16-3-19	
266.	Nettie G_____ d.10 May 1886 ae.9-3-22	

264.Manning Delia wife of James b.1834 d.1889   no more
265. Willie F_____ d.24 May 1886 ae.16-3-19
266. Nettie G_____ d.10 May 1886 ae.9-3-22

267.Merritt Henry J_____ b.1829 d.1901 no more
268. Maria Louise his wife b.1836 d.1879 no more
these two are on the same stone

269.McQuestion Mary H_____ d.9 June 1869 in 80 wife of Robert
270. Esther C_____ their daughter d.17 Sept.1851 ae.19-
-2-0

271.Mead Alice May d.24 Feb.1887 ae.26 wife of Willis T____
272. Rev.Mark d.8 Aug.1864 ae.81-9-2
273. Hannah his widow d.25 Apr.1873 ae.90-0-7
274. Sylvester (M.D.) d.21 Dec.1894 ae.88
275. Frederick G_____ C_____ b.5 Oct.1867 d.21 Dec.1905
276. Lyman d.4 Feb.1895 ae.70
277. Sarah Finette his wife d.26 July 1857 ae.27-4-27
278. Julia A_____ their daughter no date aged 1-4-0
279. Dora M_____ no date ae.0-4-23
280. Martha A_____ d.12 Nov.1875 ae.3-8-0
279 and 280 are the children of Lyman and Harriet R_
281. Henry d.1 July 1850 ae.35-10-17
282. Deborah d.12 Feb.1829 ae.17-0-19
283. Lucretia d.24 June 1830 ae.20-3-19
281 per 283 are the children of 284 and 285
284. Zenas d.9 June 1830 ae.78-6-0
285. Mary his wife d.30 Dec.1859 ae.71-4-0
286. Jonas d.24 June 1876 ae.70-7-7
287. Abigail his widow d.5 Feb.1892 ae.83-1-14
288. Emeline their daughter b.16 Nov.1836 d.16 Aug.1854
at school in Bloomfield,N.J.
289. Lockwood P_____ Clark D.6 Sept.1864 ae.45-0-9
290. Eliza his wife d.10 Apr.1880 ae.59-2-19
291. Maria A_____ Mills d.25 Oct.1885 ae.1-2-0 daughter
of George H_____ and Lucretia
271 per 291 are in a plot

292.Mead Rachel d.27 Nov.1773 ae.20-11-14 wife of Jonah

293.Merritt George E_____ d.12 Oct.1860 ae.19-1-10
294. John A_____ d.21 Apr.1861 ae.51
295. Lavina his wife d.24 Nov.1882 ae.72-7-4
296. Mary J_____ d.26 Apr.1868 ae.26-0-4 wife of J_____
P_____ Brooker

297. Merritt   Oscar d.18 Aug.1892 ae.17-1-15
298.   Anna A_____ d.4 Mch.1858 ae.2-10-2
                297 and 298 are the children of Alvah and Sarah E____
                293 per 298 are in a plot

299. Miller   Mildred J_____ b.5 May -- d.31 May -- 1903 daughter
                of Fred B_____ and Bertha A_____
300.   William G_____ d.17 Sept.1873 ae.9-4-0
301.   Lucy M_____ M_____ d.21 June 1866 ae.18-8-0 daugh-
                ter of Albert H_____ and Julia A_____
                300 and 301 are on the same stone
302.   Charles H_____ d.11 Oct.1888 ae.44-6-0
303.   Albert H_____ d.5 Mch.1893 ae.79
304.   "Jos."Edward d.30 Aug.1900 ae.42
                300 per 304 are on a monument

305. Marshall Alexander S_____ d.8.Nov.1891 ae.56 "A.F.and A.M."
                in the plot of Charles Studwell
306.   Sergt.Drake S_____ d.18 June 1867 in the army ae.26
                -5-12   of consumption
307.   Bonny S_____ d.18 Aug.1854 ae.14-4-11
308.   Sarah J_____ d.12 Sept.1845 ae.1-4-2
                307 and 308 are the children of Drake and Rebecca
309.   Rufus P_____ d.19 May 1869 ae.22-6-18
310.   Charles E_____ d.13 Feb.1877 ae.22-10-23
                309 and 310 are on the same stone
311.   Drake d.6 Oct.1863 ae.52-6-11
312.   Rebecca his wife d.19 Nov.1883 ae.72-3-18
313.   John d.19 Nov.1870 no age Co. I 17 Conn.Vols.
314.   Julia Ann b.3 Sept.1832 d.5 Apr.1841 daughter of
                John and Susan

315. Mead   Mary E_____ d.5 July 1892 ae.2-11-0 daughter of S____
                B_____ and A_____ M_____
316.   Frankie d.8 Dec.1874 ae.3 yrs. son of Z_____ and
                L_____ E_____

317. Mead   James b.1807 d.1876 no more
318.   Oliver A____ d.16 May 1854 ae.1-2-10
319.   Lizzie A____ d.11 May 1865 ae.2-7-23
320.   Arabella b.21 Mch.1851 d.26 Apr.1881
                318 per 320 are the children of Joseph G_____ and
                Mary (Taylor)
321.   Jotham Taylor d.11 Dec.1855 ae.69
                317 per 321 are in a plot

322. Mead   Amos d.24 Aug.1850 ae.69-1-7

323.Mead   Alice his wife d.17 Feb.1815 ae.29-11-7 nee Belcher
324.   Mary Purdy his wife d.1 Mch.1832 ae.37-6-0
325.   Edgar b.1830 d.aged about 3 yrs.   no more
326.   Elisha B_____ d.5 Apr.1849 ae.25-7-16
327.   Stephen W_____ d.23 Feb.1852 ae.30-6-8
           322 per 327 are in the Elkanah Mead plot ; see 341

328.Marshall Harriet J_____ d.15 Oct.1890 ae.22-10-3 daughter of
          Henry and Sarah
329.   Gilbert b.25 Dec.1827 d.18 Jan.1902
330.   Jonathan b.14 Nov.1820 d.7 Dec.1889
331.   Maria d.1 May 1899 no age
          stones 330 and 331 are exactly alike
332.   Belle d.13 Aug.1880 ae.20-3-26 only daughter of Gil-
          bert and Hannah
333.   Sarah Maria Wade wife of James W_____ d.1 Jan.1858
          ae.29-5-22 (nee ? Westcott ?)

334.Merritt Louis I_____ d.23 Dec.1906 ae.43
335.   Emma Otto his wife d.6 Oct.1889 ae.27
          these two are on the same stone

336.Mead   Hannah wife of Ebenezer d.9 Nov.1746 in 52 nee Brown
337.   Hannah only daughter of Eben b.5 Dec.1734 d.25 June
          1757 in 22
338.   Ebenezer b.25 Oct.1692 d.3 May 1775 in 83
339.   Sarah relict of Capt.Jabez d.Apr."V"1787 ae.83 nee
          Mills ; daughter of Samuel Mills
340.   "J.M." probably Capt.Jabez b.10 June 1699 d.1769
          after 3 April ; this stone is broken and is alongside
          of 339

341.Mead   Elkanah b.16 Mch.1818 d.12 Apr.1894
342.   Jane Mead his wife b.18 Apr.1817 d.28 Apr.1872
343.   Elisha Belcher d.31 July 1885 ae.1-2-20 son of Elka-
          nah and Esther W_____ (nee Waterbury)
344.   Stephen Waring d.29 Apr.1855 ae.1-9-4
345.   Catharine Lyon b.20 Aug.1842 d.31 Jan.1893
346.   Thirza Jane d.13 June 1843 ae.2-4-29 daughter of El-
          kanah and Jane
          344 per 346 are on the same stone
347.   Hannah B_____ d.11 Jan.1871 ae.26-0-21 wife of Jared
          Finch
          341. per 347 are in a plot   see 322

348.Moshier James d.24 Jan.1878 ae.68-6-5

349. Loshier   Lois his wife b.14 Dec.1814 d.5 Feb.1896 nee Timpany
                she descends from Lois Todd Mead Holly
350.   Jennie H_____ d.3 Feb.1877 ae.26-8-8 wife of Samuel
                A_____
351.   Leander b.Greenwich,Conn.1 Dec.1841 d.15 Nov.1862
                ae.20-11-15 in Newbern,N.C. Co. I 10 Conn.Vols.

352. Nichols   John A_____ d.20 Sept.1899 ae.72 Co.B,17 Conn.Vols.

     Osborn   see Christian 71 ; Dayton 100

     Otto   see Merritt 335

353. Owens   Charles W_____ d.16 Sept.1882 ae.69-10-13
354.   Mary E_____ Burns his wife d.27 Aug.1879 ae.61-5-12

     Oxer   see Ritch 403

     Park   see Husted 186

     Peck   see Denton 77 ; Peck 365 and 372 ; Ritch 404 ;
                Shute 436 ; Weed 499

     Pieffer   see Bock 42

     Pond   see Marshall 251

355. Park   William d.19 Dec.1866 ae.4-3-0

356. Peterson Robert d.15 May 1885 no,age   Co.E,29 Conn.Vols.

357. Peck   Joseph A_____ d.6 Mch.1863 ae.32-9-1
358.   "Mrs."Sarah d.27 Jan.1866 ae.65-7-9 nee Guernsey
359.   Nehemiah Lewis b.8 July 1852 d.7 Jan.1855 ae.2-6-0
                son of Alpheus and Louisa A_____ (nee Steitz)
360.   Israel d.18 Jan.1819 in 69
361.   Lavina Purdy (?his wife ?)d.12 Jan.1838 ae.82-11-9
362.   Rachel their daughter b.28 Oct.1787 d.25 Mch.1872
363.   Israel d.22 Apr.1784 ae.89-4-15
364.   Almira Mead his wife d.18 Nov.1831 ae.80-2-3

365. Peck   Dorinday wife of Israel b.20 Feb.1796 d.9 Dec.1871
                daughter of Jabez and Mary Peck
366.   Jabez d.9 Apr.1847 ae.25 son of Israel and Dorinda

367. Palmer   Hattie A_____ b.18 June 1867 d.21 Nov.1873
368.   Jennie b.10 Dec.1870 d.15 Feb.1872
                these two are the children of Darius M_____ and Harrie

369. Peck   Cornelius b.27 June 1823 d.18 Oct.1826 this stone is
                next to 381 and 382
370.   little Anna born and died 1817   no more
371.   Luther b.22 Dec.1766 d.29 Oct.1860
372.   Rachel his wife b.15 May 1775 d.2 Apr.1855 nee Peck
                371 and 372 are on the same stone

373. Peck   Eliza A_____ b.23 July-- d.11 Aug.-- 1869 daughter of
                Edward A_____ and Frances M_____
375.   Edward A_____ b.22 Oct.1834 d.12 Mch.1884
376.   Ella F_____ b.12 Sept.1870 d.10 Feb.1890
377.   Eliza J_____ Scofield b.17 May 1840 d.25 Mch.1867
378.   Leola Matilda Scofield b.30 Aug.1859 d.2 Sept.1861
379.   Joseph Henry Scofield d.28 Jan.1858 ae.5-0-3
                377 per 379 are the children of William and Cornelia
                (Mead)
380.   /Cornelia Mead b.12 Sept.1820 d.9 June 1873 wife of
                William Scofield
                373 per 380 are in a plot

381. Peck   Samuel d,21 Mch.1798 ae.59-4-27
382.   Hannah Sherwood his wife d.16 Apr.1811 ae.67-3-7

383. Partridge James Chandler d.4 Apr.1898 ae.1 year son of C_____
                R_____ and A_____ L_____

Purdy   see Mead 324 ; Peck 361

Ray   see Cameron 58 ; Ferguson 122 and 123 and 124

Rich   see Studwell 452

Roswell   see Ingersoll 187

Rubindin see Morton 228

384.Radford	Francis d.12 Sept.1574 ae.32
385.	Barbara his wife d.2 Mch.1875 ae.22-0-22
386.Reed	Ephraim d.6 Mch.1874 ae.55-1-15
387.Reynolds	Henrietta R_____ d.8 Feb.1882 ae.23-0-8 wife of Charles
388.	Mary J_____ Stephens b.30 Dec.1825 d.6 Jan.1890 wife of William H_____
389.	Willie Everett Delano d.31 Mch.1822 ae.4-9-22
390.	Howard Delano d.23 July 1876 ae.0-8-22
	389 and 390 are the children of W___ _ S_____ and S_____ E_____.
391.Rodermond	Michael C_____ b.25 Dec.1826 d.23 Oct.1885
392.	Jane his wife b.16 May 1835 d.1 Apr.1889
	these two are in a plot
393.Ritch	Sarah d.7 Aug.1388 ae.60-11-25 wife of William M****
394.	Ralph their son d.11 July 1856 ae.4 days
395.	Sarah E_____ b.12 June 1851 d.18 Sept.1892
396.	Clara L_____ d.3 Mch.1899 ae.10-2-25
397.	Harry W_____ d.11 Sept.1885 ae.1-8-24
	396 and 397 are the children of Willis M_____ and Lillie
398.	Lyman M_____ d.15 July 1885 ae.0-10-1
399.	Mabel H_____ d.14 Apr.1890 ae.2-3-4
	398 and 399 are the children of Silas D_____ and Ida F_____
400.	George H_____ b.23 Aug.1852 d.9 Jan.1896
401.	Bobby b.24 June-- d.8 July-- 1885
402.	Ada D_____ d.2 Nov.1892 ae.3 yrs.
	401 and 402 are the children of George H_____ and Susie D_____
	Robert P_____ Mead 220 here
403.	William R_____ Oxer d.2 Nov.1873 ae.30-11-3
404.	Emma M_____ Ritch d.20 May 1883 ae.28-10-0 wife of Elias D_____ Peck
405.	Hudson L_____ b.5 Apr.1888 ae.27-6-29
406.	Thomas b.14 Jan.1825 d.22 Apr.1904
407.	Elizabeth his first wife d.10 Dec.1856 ae.22-9-28
408.	Sarah F_____ his second wife d.13 Mch.1872 ae.32-4--20
409.	Louise S_____(or D_____)his third wife b.29 June 1834 d.8 Oct.1894
410.	Ralph d.28 Dec.1846 ae.48-9-9
411.	Clemence S_____ Mead his wife d.27 Mch.1867 ae.69-3-2

412.Ritch   Justus d.5 July 1864 ae.42-5-21
413.   Frances A_____ Ritch d.26 Jan.1856 ae.29-0-1? wife
             of John Blackett
             393 per 413 are all in one plot

414.Rowe   William M_____ b.21-- d.28---June 1894
415.   George b.28 June 1897 d.18 June 1903
416.   Sarah b.21 Nov.1902 d.1 Jan.1903

417.St.John Alice F_____ d.18 Aug.1863 ae.3-11-1
418.   Frederick A_____ d.27 Nov.1864 ae.0-11-23
             417 and 418 are the children of Albert G_____ and
             Sarah E_____
419.   Sarah E_____ d.12 Feb.1872 ae.36 daughter of John
             and Mary A_____ Ferris

420.Sampson Augustus b.9 Sept.1830 d.20 Sept.1883
421.   Ida May b.10 Aug.1867 d.19 Sept.1872
             these two are in a plot

422.Sargent Moses F_____ d.29 Mch.1862 ae.2-10-3 son of Moses F__
             and Mary J_____

     Saunders see Worden 523

     Scofield see Ingersoll 187 ; Peck 377 per 380

423.Scofield Sylvester M_____ b.12 June 1876 d.1 June 1886
424.   Maud d.20 Aug.1883 ae.0-5-7
425.   Julia D_____ d.1 June 1878,ae.0-4-14
             these three are the children of George E_____ and
             Isabel C_____
426.   George A_____ b.6 July 1868 d.7 Oct.1904 "A.F.and
             A.M."
427.   Alford V_____ B_____ b.21 Feb.1838 d.31 Jan.1898
             "G.A.R."
428.   Rufus d.28 July 1854 ae.75 see the large 3 volume
             Whitney Genealogy for his descendants

429.Scott   Capt.William d.13 July 1899 ae.87
430.   Mary E_____ his wife d.29 Oct.1877 ae.60
431.   Charles E_____ b.1843 d.1900 no more

     Scudder see Howard 155

432.Seward Sadie d.9 Apr.1887 ae.33 wife of James H_____

433.Shea Marion A_____ d.6 June 1870 ae.0-2-10
434. Sarah T_____ d.6 Mch.1872 ae.0-6-16
these two are the children of James and Sarah E____

Sherwood see Chase 52 and 55 ; Lent 206 ; Peck 382

435.Shute Gilbert b.8 Feb.1814 d.21 Apr.1883 ae.69-2-15
436. Mary Peck his wife b.12 July 1820 d.24 Mch.1867

Simmons see Stoothoff 450

437.Slagle Isabella b.19 May 1842 d.16 Dec.1880 wife of Sullivan W_____

438.Slater M_____ Augusta b.5 Jan.1850 d.10 May 1901

439.Slocum Cynthia d.16 Sept.1877 ae.62-10-19 wife of James W___

440.Smith Mildred A_____ d.1 June 1902 no more
441. Ellen d.5 Jan.1880 in 72
442. Carleton Hoyt d.6 July 1878 ae.10 mos. son of Mortimer F_____ and Libbie

Smith see Hubbard 164 ; Studwell 451

443.Sniffen Charles W_____ d.18 June 1856 ae.36-8-9 eldest son of Epenetus and Hulda

444.this stone was down and too heavy to lift
445.this stone was down and too heavy to lift

446.Sniffen Jennie d.6 Feb.1856 ae.0-9-20 infant daughter of Samuel L_____ and Maria

Spencer see Johnson 190

Steitz see Peck 359

Stephens   see Reynolds 388

447.Stevens   Grace b.25 Apr.1893 d.14 Apr.1898 daughter of
Frank and Emma (Marshall) ; this stone is
near the Studwell plot

448.Stevenson   Edward d.15 Sept.1795 ae.20-7-0 son of Frederick

449.Stoothoff   Stephen A_____   no dates
450.   Susan Simmons his wife b.23 May 1828 d.21 Aug.1905

Studwell   see Marshall 305 ; Stevens 445

451.Studwell   Sarah E_____ d.20 Jan.1899 ae.58 daughter of
Luther Harvey Studwell and Julia (Ferris)
Luther H. was son of Drake and Elizabeth (Smith)
452.   Capt.Charles d.31 Dec.1868 ae.62-3-12 son of Solomon and Esther (Rich)
453.   Margaret Ann Bunker his wife d.16 Mch.1860 ae.
50-8-15

454.Studwell   Caroline L_____ June d.9 Jan.1875 ae.36-4-8 wife
of Charles E_____
455.   Margaret B_____ their daughter b.26 Oct.1866 d.18
Mch.1897
456.   Bertha I_____ d.9 Jan.1875 ae.5-0-11
457.   Mamie Hyatt d.23 Aug.1868 ae.0-5-28
458.   Carrie Jane d.18 Nov.1865 ae.0-4-18
455 per 458 are the children of Charles E_____
and Caroline L_____
454 per 458 are in a plot

459.Studwell   Capt.Henry F_____ b.22 July 1813 d.24 May 1884
460.   Amanda Barnacutt his wife b.29 June 1819 d.9
Mch.1872
these two are on a monument
461.   Frank B_____ d.29 Oct.1884 ae.28-5-25
462.   Susan A_____ d.21 Aug.1850 ae.2-4-0
463.   William H_____ b.29 May 1843 d.16 Sept.1894
461 per 464 are the children of 459 and 460
464.   Alice M_____ b.3 July 1873 d.28 Apr.1896 daughter of John K_____ and Isabella A_____
(Telfer)
459 per 464 are in a plot

465.Studwell   George O_____ b.3 Dec. 1817 d.__ __ 1897 no more
466.   Joanna Buckhout his wife b.1816 d.1 Dec.1866 ae.
                    50-1-0 daughter of James
467.   Margaret Buckhout his second wife b.1821 d.1867
                    no more   she does not appear in "The Studwell
                    Family of Fairfield County,Conn." 1899
                    these three are on a monument
468.   John Henry d.9 Nov.1866 in 18 year
469.   Henrietta H_____ Townsend b.1 Dec.1867 d.8 Aug.1868
470.   Herbert Henry Townsend d.30 June 1872 ae.1-1-3
471.   Bertha Eugenia Townsend d.30 Mch.1881 ae.3-2-21
472.   Henrietta Anna Townsend d.25 Mch.1881 ae.7-9-4
                    471 and 472 are on a monument
                    469 per 472 are the children of George S_____
                    and Henrietta B_____ (Studwell)
                    465 per 472 are in a plot

        Sydney   see Lockwood 209

473.Talbot   George E_____ b.1856 d.1896 no more
474.   Virginia his wife b.1865 d.1893 no more
                    these two are on the same stone
475.   baby Louie no date aged 0-4-26 no more
476.   William d.20 Jan.1884 ae.58-11-19 "Father"
477.   Chester b.11 Aug.1880 d.28 Sept.1887 son of W____
                    R_____ and A_____ A_____

        Taylor   see Mead 320 and 321

        Telfer   see Studwell 464

478.Tilson   Zachariah L_____ d.28 June 1905 ae.1-6-2 son of
                Edward G_____ and Emma F_____

        Timpany   see Moshier 349 ; Worden 523

479.Timpany   Elvira d.10 Nov.1880 ae.78-10-14
480.   Charles d.27 Oct.1889 ae.72-8-27
481.   Delia A_____ his wife d.18 Aug.1893 ae.73-8-4
482.   Hannah d.1 Oct.1861 ae.39-5-23

        Townsend   see Studwell 469 per 472 ;

        Todd   see Moshier 349

483.	Trowbridge	Clara B_____ no more
484.		Lily no more
485.		Willie no more
486.		James no more

these four are on the same stone ; 484 per 486 are
are the children of Clara B_____

487.	Turner	Edward Frank b.1863 d.1900 no more
488.		Ella L_____ Morrell his wife b.1861 d.1902 no more
489.		Edward E_____ their son d.6 May 1894 ae.0-23-2

490.	Voss	Charles A_____ d.17 Apr.1866 ae.22-3-25
491.		John Henry d.2 Aug.1875 ae.68-3-12

Wade   see Marshall 333

Wallace   see Hubbard 164 ; Morrell 229

492.	Wallace	William d.5 Jan.1884 ae.70
493.		Eliza his wife d.18 June 1900 ae.84

these two are on a monument

494.		William H_____ b.27 Dec.1839 d,4 Apr.1906

495. Walz   Elizabeth b.8 May 1838 d.27 Apr.1904 wife of
Louis

Waring   see Mead 344

Warren   see Mead 240

Waterbury   see Mead 343

496. Watson   Jennie d.20 Oct.1873 ae.24-8-6 wife of L____ ___
E_____

Webb   see Carr 56

Webber   see Ingersoll 187

497. Weber   Margaret d.27 Mch.1868 ae.23-0-28 wife of John

498.Weed   Isaac b.15 Feb.1802 d.30 Jan.1897

499.   Huldah Peck his wife b.27 Apr.1802 d.18 Aug.1891

500.   Emily their daughter d.24 Aug.1834 ae.0-9-19

501.   Edwin G_____ d.15 Mch.1869 ae.3-9-10 son of Edwin
            P_____ and Celine C_____

502.   Isaac d.20 May 1831 ae.76-11-15

503.   Hannah his wife d.6 Feb.1838 ae.76-6-15

504.Weiss   Charles d.4 Nov.1893 ae.52

505.Wescott   John b.10 May 1800 d.14 May 1879

506.   Elizabeth his wife d.14 June 1862 ae.59-1-11

     Westcott see Marshall 333

507.White   William b.18 June 1816 d.23 Nov.1868 "Father"

508.   Elizabeth b.1 July 1817 d.9 Aug.1875 "Our Mother"
          these two are on a monument

509.   Benjamin their son d.17 July 1875 ae.16-8-0

510.   Emeline d.18 Sept.1843 ae.10 mos.

511.   William Henry d.4 Aug.1844 ae.0-3-20

512.   Thomas d.3 Nov.1845 ae.0-4-23

513.   Jane d.6 Apr.1846 ae.9-6-20
          510 per 513 are on a monument

     Whitney   see Scofield 428

514.Wiegand   Ida R_____ d.8 Oct.1885 ae.26-9-10 wife of J_____
            H_____

     Wilber   see Luther 205

     Willis   see Mead 271

515.Wilmot   Joseph d.30 May 1868 ae.69

516.   Mary his wife d.3 Apr.1872 ae.66

517.Wilson   Thomas d.9 Jan.1860 ae.65-0-28

518.Worden   E_____ B_____ b.28 May 1833 d.26 Aug.1904 "Father"

519.Worden	Hannah M_____ d.16 Mch.1868 ae.30-6-16	
520.	this stone sunken	
521.	Andrew d.19 Jan.1868 ae.64-9-0 son of Isaac and Hannah	
522.	Amanda Timpany his wife b.27 Aug.1808 d.5 Feb.1886	
523.	Hannah d.26 Jan.1853 ae.81-7-7 wife of Isaac ; probably nee Saunders	

Wright   see Carter 67 and 68

The oldest stone is Nov.1746 Hannah (Brown) Mead 336
The latest stone is Dec.1906 Louis I_____ Merritt 334

Notes

200.Lyon   Algernon Bouton b.14 July 1855 d._ _ 1897 son of
Augustus S_____ and Elizabryh Betts (Bouton)

201.   David son of David and Elizabeth (Townsend)

202.   Elizabeth M____ Jones daughter of James and Elizabeth

174.Hecker   b.24 Aug.1895 son of Frederick M_____ b.2 Aug.1874
married 22 July 1894 Lena R_____ Mead b.18 Mch.1873
daughter of Bush and Sarah (Wilson)

238.Mead   Amos son of Matthew and Nancy (Hobby)

239.   Mary Eliza Stryker

240.   b.6 Jan.1865

241.   b.6 Apr.1861

242.   Matthew b.3 Mch.1814 married July __1852 ; son of
Bush and Sarah (Wilson)

243.   Mary Bush b.23 Sept.1813 married first Hiram Ray

262.Matthews John married Susan Mead b._____ daughter of Bush
and Sarah (Wilson)

258.Merritt Nancy (nee Hobby) Mead ; Hannah b.6 July 1791

220.Mead   Robert P____son of Lucknor and Sophia (Fletcher)

276.Mead   Lyman b.26 Mch.1824 married 18 Sept.1848 Sarah F____
Acker ; son of Zenas and Mary (Lashly)

306.Marshall Drake S____ b.5 Dec.1841 son of Drake b.20 Mch.1811
married 21 Mch.1832 Rebecca Mead b.31 July 1811 daughter of Justus B_____ and Polly (Knapp)

307.   Benny S_____ b.2 Apr.1840

308.   b.10 May 1844

309.   b.1 Nov.1846

310.   b.20 Mch.1854
309 and 310 are the children of Drake and Rebecca (Mead)

338.Mead   Ebenezer son of Ebenezer and Sarah (Knapp)
he married second 19 Dec.1759 in the Congregational
Church in New Canaan,Conn.,Naomi Weed ; she survived
him

339.   Sarah daughter of Samuel and Sarah (Denton) Mills

Notes ; page 2

383.Partridge   James C. son of Charles R____ b.28 July 1867 married 27 June 1894 Adeline L_____ Mead b.23 Feb.1867 daughter of Zachariah and Louisa E_____ (Welch)

393.Ritch   nee Sarah Hamilton
William M____ b.1 June 1824 son of Ralph and Clemence (Mead)

396.   Willis M_____ b.15 Sept.1835 married Elizabeth Henderson

398.   Silas D_____ married Ida F_____ Mead daughter of Lyman and Harriet R_____ (Mead)

405.   Hudson L____b.7 Sept.1860 married 11 Aug.1886 Harriet J_____ Mead b.26 May 1863 son of Thomas and Sarah F_____ (Silleck)

406.   Thomas son of Ralph and Clemence (Mead)

407.   Elizabeth A_____ Silleck married 30 Jan.1854

408.   Sarah F_____ Silleck married 9 Jan.1858

409.   Mrs.Louise S____ Mead married 3 Aug.1873 ; she was widow of Major Daniel M_____ Mead ; daughter of Col. Thomas and Hannah (Seaman) Mead ; Thomas Ritch married fourth 1 June 1896 Evalyn Cramer

411.   Clemence S.b.25 Dec.1797 married 5 Dec.1819 ; daughter of Matthew and Nancy (Hobby) Mead

412.   Justus b.14 Jan.1822 married Maria Rodeman

413.   Frances A. b.14 Jan.1831 married first Capt.William Peck ; married second John Sackett

417.St.John   Albert Gould b.28 Nov.1830 d.Feb.__1878son of Gould Lee St,John and Esther Mary (Lockwood) ; A.G.married Elizabeth Ferris b.7 Mch.1836 ; John Ferris married Mary Amanda Forbes ; Alice F. b.17 Sept.1859

418.   Frederick Almon b.4 Dec.1863

423.Scofield   William b.20 Sept.1815 d.10 Apr.1885 married Feb.___ 1838 Cornelia Mead (see 380) and had George b.29 Jan 1848 married 19 Oct.1870 Isabel C____Merritt b.16 June 1852

Index page 2

Index page 5

Index page 7